SPIRIT MACHINES

POETRY

A Scottish Assembly
Sharawaggi (with W. N. Herbert)
Talkies
Masculinity
Penguin Modern Poets 9 (with John Burnside and Kathleen Jamie)

ANTHOLOGIES

ed., *Other Tongues*
ed., with Simon Armitage, *The Penguin Book of Poetry from Britain
and Ireland since 1945*

CRITICISM

The Savage and the City in the Work of T. S. Eliot
Devolving English Literature
Identifying Poets: Self and Territory in Twentieth-Century Poetry
Literature in Twentieth-Century Scotland
ed., with Hamish Whyte, *About Edwin Morgan*
ed., with Thom Nairn, *The Arts of Alasdair Gray*
ed., with David Kinloch, *Reading Douglas Dunn*
ed., with Anne Varty, *Liz Lochhead's Voices*
ed., with Henry Hart, David Kinloch and Richard Price, *Talking
Verse: Interviews with Poets*
ed., *Robert Burns and Cultural Authority*
ed., *Launch-site for English Studies*
ed., *The Scottish Invention of English Literature*

SPIRIT MACHINES

Robert Crawford

CAPE POETRY

First published 1999

1 3 5 7 9 10 8 6 4 2

First published in the United Kingdom in 1999 by Jonathan Cape,
Random House, 20 Vauxhall Bridge Road, London SW1V 2SA

Random House Australia (Pty) Limited
20 Alfred Street, Milsons Point, Sydney,
New South Wales 2061, Australia

Random House New Zealand Limited
18 Poland Road, Glenfield,
Auckland 10, New Zealand

Random House South Africa (Pty) Limited
Endulini, 5A Jubilee Road, Parktown 2193, South Africa

Random House UK Limited Reg. No. 954009

A CIP catalogue record for this book is available from the British Library

Papers used by Random House UK Limited are natural,
recyclable products made from wood grown in sustainable forests.
The manufacturing processes conform to the environmental
regulations of the country of origin.

ISBN 0-224-05901-7

Typeset by Palimpsest Book Production Limited,
Polmont, Stirlingshire
Printed and bound in Great Britain
by Creative Print and Design (Wales), Ebbw Vale

for Alice, Lewis, and Blyth

with love

CONTENTS

ACKNOWLEDGEMENTS

I would like to thank the editors of the following journals where some of these poems have appeared: *Balliol College Annual Record, Comparative Criticism, The Herald, Janus, Landfall, London Review of Books, Notre Dame Review, Poetry Review, The Scotsman, Soho Square VII, The Red Wheelbarrow, Times Literary Supplement, Verse*. The sequence 'Spirit Machines' was commissioned and produced by Tim Dee of BBC Radio 3 and a version of it was broadcast as a programme in 1997. I owe a debt to Elisabeth Jay and Penny Fielding for their writings about Margaret Oliphant. I am grateful to Tony Delamothe of the *British Medical Journal* who wrote to me pointing out some medical problems in 'A Life-Exam'.

'Impossibility' appeared as a limited-edition artist's book in collaboration with the etcher Caroline Saltzwedel and was published by Hirundo Press, Hamburg, in 1998.

POLLEN

POLLENATION

In a Corrievreckan of navy blues
Going down in the west

Hail seethes round your
Ports of mouth-music and horses' graves;

Landfall winds a salty chant
Antiphonal among peatsmoke.

Clogging thatched roots, dampened masses
Meld with bleared weather and mellow lowing of cows;

Jetsam off jetsam, needle's eye-land,
Hallucinatory *hi ro, ho ro*,

Downpoured through heat's bodiless shimmer,
The first cell of Columba.

Here the great presbyterian minister
With his lifeboat and memorial lighthouse

Sails with the captain of many clippers
Towards the Salutation Bar.

Herring gulls take off. Terns loop down to us striding
On slime-green steppingstones over the dreel

Under a clear, bespectacled sky
Crowstepped with masonic symbols.

Where the Beggar's Benison met to measure their pricks
On a special platter, we stand and stare up at the stars

Near the electrician's. They look so close
They should be catching lobsters and called

Not the Plough but Breadwinner III,
Shearwater of Cellardyke, North Carr Lightship,

Morning Ray, Fisher of Men.
High above piers and long breakwaters

They trawl dour, intergalactic North Seas,
Making pantiles sparkle and cornfields with tubular stooks

Harvested in farmtouns beyond Anstruther
Wink in their great moderator's eye

Overseeing his congregation
As they sing in a tethered boat that is bobbing

Down and up, gently
Up and down.

SOBIESKI-STUARTS

On scuffed chaise-longues in Europe's drawing-rooms
Sobieski-Stuarts audition for thrones.

Their Gaelic is not the Gaelic of Borrodale
But the Gaelic of Baden-Baden.

Draped in ancient, oddly pristine
Manic-depressive tartans,

Soi-distant with calipered wrists,
Statuesque for early cameras,

Soon they pirouette to receive
Double malts and weary autograph hunters,

Couples rubicundly stripping the willow
After the band has gone home.

Trains connect for the Hook of Holland,
Luxembourg, St Germain.

Underneath heavy evening cloud
The sun sets, a jabot of light.

THE DESCENT

(S.J.B., *1957–1995*)

Roped to myself, I inched away
Down towards a bottle-dungeon where
Dank slabs forgot the normal day.
Inside it, knotted with despair,

I laughed and told my cleverest jokes,
I told the best jokes, I was told
My bottle-dungeon was a hoax
I'd see through, if I just grew old.

Sometimes I am the Joycean face,
The cobbled street you drift along,
The video shop, the tashed briefcase,
The tenor breaking into song

In Gaelic or Italian, 'Oh!'
Stroke your baby in his cot,
His curls, his skin-folds that will grow
Smoothed out. I have to cut this knot.

THE BOYS

In the chapel at Stephen's memorial service
I saw his two wee boys across the aisle

Like dolls. Their mother had her arms around them.
One of them started singing 'Happy Birthday'

At the benediction. Afterwards, he told me
How they'd holidayed at Butlin's, riding donkeys

And a motorbike. He tugged a grey, felt hippo
With very small ears, abruptly started laughing,

Then crying out, just shouting for his brother,
'Wayhayhayhayhayhayhayhayhayhay!'

Across the formal, patterned, deep-pile carpet
Among dark-suited and dark-stockinged legs.

THE RESULT

1707–1997; for Alice

Moments after death, I found my voice
Surprising, hearing my own

Ansafone saying, 'I'm not here just now,
Please speak after the tone.'

You saw it in my eyes – release
Back to the world. More, more

You, Scotland, sea, each lost and re-elected.
I toast debatable lands, the come-go shore

Of living here. 'Thanks!' My full, bannock-smeared glass
Rises to you, our son, and our new, blonde

Daughter. We dance, in grey St Michael slippers,
Cancerless, broken out, and passed beyond.

BALANCE

If one thing in the balance for the day
Did not pan out exactly, they'd work on

Underneath a dusty chandelier.
Bankerly, penned columns made a picture

Whose hatch and nuance summed up everything
But wasn't right. Exhausted, carried-over

Figures crouched in endless long divisions.
Tellers slogged towards the perfect balance

That healed the night, releasing all its workers
To branch-line stations where their journey times

Shortened and shortened until negative numbers
Jammed the timetable, the next scheduled service

Insolubly delayed and gone already,
Nudging the buffers long before its start.

RELIEF

New boy at the Union Bank of Scotland,
Dad was often asked to do relief

In country branches. He would take a shotgun
To the Manager's Office, swivelling in his chair,

Both barrels resting on the windowsill.
He blasted rabbits. Sometimes customers,

Jumping at the 'whump!' behind yon hardwood door,
Asked for the manager. A clerk sent Dad

Down the hidden bank-house garden where Old Grant
Strained with a spade, lifting his new potatoes.

He'd straighten, yank the hip-flask from his pocket,
Take a long swig until his chin relaxed

Above his quickly retied tie, then stroll
Back to his office, greet the customer

Who grinned with deliverance, the way Dad did
When I asked abruptly, 'Where was the bank with the rabbits?'

In his last year, he told me, like a shot,
'Aberlour on Speyside, near to Grantown.'

I knew he was the only one alive
Knew the right answer. Now I have relieved him.

THE SOPHISTICATE

I am a tall, mid-Western gynaecologist
Arrived in Paris for my very first time,

Sure it's a city of the imagination
Solid as this kerb in Montparnasse.

Patisseries, deep spinach roulades, wines,
Dark-varnished shelves of petites tartes oignons –

I buy a hat, a small cigar, and then,
Stepping up to give my keynote speech,

I clearly see its thirty numbered pages
Locked in the third drawer down, left far behind me

In Iowa, or dour Lincoln, Nebraska,
Second Pond, Joesville, or Junction Gulch.

Visiting, I was back in the old country.
Red sandstone tenements, top flats called Lochnagar,

Where my host from the Scottish Hellenic Society
Asked in his high-ceilinged guest-bedroom,

'Will the clock disturb you?' Thinking it might,
He reached out and stopped the pendulum.

Camp-bedded under coffin bookshelves
Numismatically neat,

In between *The Scottish Coinage*
And *The Memoirs of Heinrich Schliemann*

I dreamed my nation's classical sources,
Sealed below Hyndland, waited unreduced,

Shelves sedimented with properispomenal tomes,
Trojan Spielberg, uninjured coins

Brushed clean in each layer, groats and mint pounds Scots.
Somewhere near, in an amphitheatre,

My old Greek lecturer rhotacized
(Manic hair grey now, arms all-go)

About Marathon, Marathon, the Plain of Marathon,
Book flapping up and down in the air,

A tattered flag, or the wings of a bird
That might fly off and perch somewhere else.

KNOWLEDGE

Ferrier invents the word *epistemology*
Sitting in a doorway wiped across with light

From an early flashgun. Round him, young buck students
Scatter in the aftershock, vanish.

⭐

Euclidean rain stots on cobbles
In wintry St Andrews. Ferrier hunches with cold,

Drawing his black gown over his head
Like a photographer, abolishing himself.

⭐

A sore has developed, a gland gone syphilitic.
He reads up the chemistry of mercuric oxide,

Hears his Aunt Susan, the famous author
Of *Marriage*, has died in her sleep.

⭐

Frail, he blocks a lecture-room entrance.
A New Woman confronts him: 'I wish to know

By what right you keep me from these Chemistry lectures.'
He can't move, at one with the stone.

COLUMBAN

Dawn's fractured bone
Windchills your channels,

Small, remote radio stations
Broadcasting Christ to the waves.

Your held note's
Hearing-aid whine draws congregations

Aboard ferries and over causeways.
Steelworks are flailing through the oceans,

Dirtying them as they migrate.
Dying patients, the newborn in incubators

Each have their own long, caring numbers,
Tags on the red legs of birds.

*

If a nuclear sub's
Viking blush passes down the islands,

Embarrassing Harris, North Uist, Benbecula,
Humiliating their stones,

I will mount a search. I will put to sea
Towards yon shepherd's crook of psalms,

Community's tough-minded holy grit
Round which an anchor transformed to pearl

Shines across so-called Dark Ages
Its sol-fa brecbennach of calm.

PASSAGE

in memory of John Lorne Campbell and for Margaret Fay Shaw

'Record me,' she laughs through her Gaelic dance-steps
While the cylinder reeling round and round
Scratches itself with song.

Old women's brittle notes are held
On nerve-thin, tautened Ediphone wire,
A longitude of music

Stretched in one unending passage
From the Isle of Canna to Nova Scotian
Tape-hiss of wind on snow

Where the gone-away, digitized pew by pew,
Climb aboard long tunes outlasting lips
Danced down into the machine.

GALILEE

Castor and Pollux, Cupar and Balmullo,
Cassiopeia, Blebo, Pittenweem

Cluster in needlepoint beside big planets,
Constellations, Kinshaldy and The Plough.

One with Ecurie Ecosse, the Flying Scotsman,
My soul is awkwardly solidified,

Mixed up with wireless sets and satellite junk
Floating forever. My hypermarket prayer

Asks for tired arms to reach up from my body,
Shake off credit cards, leaflets, and then

While the spirit un-numbs, and a Phoenix Choir
Rehearses songs it cannot yet get right,

Undo my spreadsheet mindset like Ned Kelly
Hauling off his heavy metal head.

I put out from the land in a great vessel
I did not make, and do not understand.

The insane, flensed face of Lord Beeching as he slashes the axe at my grandmother, blind, ninety-odds, listening to the Open University in her tea-cosy, knitted, summer hat; at my aunt, Grace Lyon, in Balfron, where she tries topiary and speaks out for a freer Scotland. Redder when he smacks the blade through my uncle, John Branwell Crawford, despite all my uncle's constabulary wiles, his versifying, his Glasgow-trained, crewcut head. Enraged and hacking bonily at my father after his operation, pursuing him from sea to sea, felling him in his own front room. Passing like the shadow of the Enola Gay over country stations, Crail and St Andrews, Musselburgh, Selkirk, their peed-in waiting-room fireplaces his memorials, their downed bridges his headstones, their deathcamp-dull railway lines his *Times* obituary, their sleeper after sleeper his death-throes in the House of Lords. The reeling, vampire-terror of Beeching as he nightly buzzes the living, his screaming acceleration when he hurtles over Pittenweem. Sometimes he flies with a bone-gaunt Margaret Thatcher, slashing and splintering, Goyaesquely devouring bagged limbs. Sometimes he goes solo, scattering plague saliva, cursed at forever, his name meaning one thing only. Unable to rest, he is chased where there are no railways, where trains never ran, down corries and through the high cols. His pursuers, aboard the Flying Scotsman, taunt him forever with soot and furnace flames, timetables, loco numbers and the screaming of great steam whistles. 'Death, thou shalt die! Death, thou shalt die!' their yells beat against the limousine of his skull.

The ritual of the taxi ride to my uncle's funeral, its names Leuchars, Pitlessie, Blairgowrie, Kippen, Balfron.

Passing a village shop whose window reads YOU CAN'T TOP TUNNOCKS, I save the striped wrapper of a Tunnock's Caramel Wafer.

All my family are graduates of that chocolate coating, loyal to its sticky texture on the teeth.

MORE THAN 4,000,000 OF THESE BISCUITS MADE AND SOLD EVERY WEEK.

I remember a claustrophobic pub behind Christ Church, Oxford, its four sides and ceiling cased with wall-to-wall, public-school ties.

My aunt's name on the gravestone surprises me. Her name was Grace Lyon. She voted for Scottish independence.

As I confusedly take a cord at my uncle's burial it is brilliantly sunny. I dream of a tabernacle of caramel and flame.

When I was a child my uncle drove us in his green, rusting Austin A30, once or twice to 'the only Lake in Scotland'.

We sailed over on the ferry to the central island with its ruined priory, near the other island where the Scottish kings stabled their hounds.

On the way home the silent taxi driver goes slowly. I know he is trying not to catch up with my uncle's now empty hearse.

BEREAVEMENT

I walk the same roads far ahead of you,
So slowly, but you never catch me up.

Your stick, homing from Market Street to South Street,
Takes you away a slightly different route.

I peer in windows at your lost reflection,
Catching you looking through me, out to sea.

We haunt each other, almost happily,
Until each sinks back into his real world,

Children dismounted from tonight's last train
At the wrong station, who can hear

Carriages that went ahead without them
Decades ago, still singing in the rails.

A LIFE-EXAM

A LIFE-EXAM

Answer truthfully from your own heart:

1. Rewrite *The Waste Land* using only
   English words of one syllable.

2. Rearrange the entire Bible
   into two columns, one headed
   KNOWLEDGE, the other WISDOM.

3. How many women did Henry VIII
   fancy, apart from his wives?

4. Make one of the following dramatic entrances:
   Natural, Caesarean, Episiotomy.

5. While breathing regularly,
   count up your limbs and cry.

6. COMPLETE EITHER SENTENCE:

   Love comes before a fall in
   Love conquers all in
   Love-in . . .

   OR

   I love . . .

7. Knit together the plates of your skull correctly.

8. Successfully avoid all of the following:
   cot-death, meningitis, heart-defects,
   leukemia, projectile vomiting, polio
   (continued in the third volume)

9. Relax.

10. Negotiate the almost simultaneous sale
    of your present home, mortgage arrangements,
    the purchase of another, roomier dwelling
    in exceptional order, a minor illness,
    a break-in, and giving birth.

11. Fall in love with a refugee
    from a completely different culture,
    whose parents are clearly, kindly against you
    and who wants to move to America.

12. Have you broken the following Ten Commandments?
    Answer each just yes or no.

13. Escape from this trap.

14. Record honestly your own feelings
    before hearing from your surgeon
    the Pathology Lab's full report
    on your sample of tissue excised.

15. Fill this bottle with urine/semen/tears.

16. Realise while in another country
    you should have married someone you knew quite well back
    home.

17. Act on this.

18. Without aid of a calculator, Napier's Bones,
    parent, child, or prior instruction,
    emulate ancient arithmeticians'
    calculations of pi.

19. Grow a tree. Manufacture a light bulb.
    Weave a carpet. Make paper. Be humble.

20. Rewrite at least one of the following:
    Kipling's 'If', your National Health Number,
    the official birthdays of the Royal family,
    your vaccination details, your unchosen names.

22. Which of the following is incorrect?
    The New Testament; The Gitas; The Koran.

23. To whom is each of these most important?
    Hitler, Jesus, Greta Garbo, you.

24. With a view to bioengineering
    suggest at least six names for new animals.

25. Imagine your reaction to the news
    that all the technologies of your childhood
    are utterly outmoded junk.

26. Preserve these four fashion items:
    flared trousers, nose rings, moustaches, clones.

27. Try to understand the laws of physics.

28. If appropriate, break your voice here.

29. Describe accurately the following diagram:

30. Now draw a diagram of your own:

31. How many words can be made from letters of the Western alphabets?

32. Catch and cook lunch.

33. While estimating the atomic weights
    of trichloroethylene
    and palladium plus mendelevium
    work out if the one in the corner fancies you.

34. Attend a funeral.

35. Die.

36. Describe the onset of your first period.

OR

Avoid this subject entirely.

37. Describe a new ritual appropriate to
    EITHER masturbation OR the purchase of a used car.

38. Write a poem in the style of Homer, beginning
    'If I won the National Lottery . . .'

39. Make love.

40. Do not read *Finnegans Wake*.

41. Which of the following domestic items
    seems to you most useful for the practice of augury?
    tealeaves; crazy paving; used nappies.

42. If you were given your chance again
    which three questions might you answer differently?

43. Name several people who found the New World.

44. Name several people who lost it.

45. 'God is love.' Discuss.

46. Who would you most like to meet?
    the inventor of the guillotine;
    the inventor of the repeating rifle;
    the inventor of toilet paper.

47. Which independent country has as its capital
    Reykjavik; Harare; Dublin; Edinburgh?

48. If allowed your own private army,
    would it comprise *a)* your immediate family,
    b) your town, *c)* the complement
    of a modest nuclear submarine, or
    d) 500 million souls?

49. Should your life become the subject
    of a soap opera, would the audience find it
    a) amusing, *b)* triumphant, *c)* compulsively watchable,
    or *d)* none of the above?

50. Describe your spiritual exercise regime.

51. Write about the (non-financial) disadvantages of early retirement.

52. Propose an original toast.

53. If you had to choose to be a forest fruit
    which would you be and why?

54. Construct a c.v. dealing with all areas of your life
    other than those of work.

55. Produce Freudian, Jungian, and Thatcherite analyses of yourself.

56. Now analyse yourself in terms of your favourite religion.

57. Write an essay called 'My Own Environmental Achievements'.

58. Summarize in 10 words the history of your greatest love.

59. Where do you see yourself in fifty years' time?

60. Think about water.

61. Could you tell by the syllabic patterns
    of names of people you met how much
    they would come to mean in your life?

62. Could you tell by bumps, angularities,
    and other phrenological signs
    on heads of people you met how much
    they would come to mean in your life?

63. Could you tell by looking at the clothes
    of people you met how much they would mean in your life?

64. Could you tell just by the sex
    of people you met how much they would mean in your life?

65. Could you tell by looking deeply
    into the eyes of people you met
    how much they would mean in your life?

66. List a hundred personal possessions
    you could readily do without.

67. Now list a further hundred.

68. What is the question you'd most like to have asked
    and never dared to answer?

69. Write here the names of those you pray for.

70. Write here to whom you pray.

71. From here on you may add optional questions, and need not
    supply answers.

    (Success or failure in the above paper will inevitably lead to riches
    or poverty; define these in your own terms.)

    NOTES

HIGHLAND POEMS

No more shall he hear thy voice like the sound of the string of music.
The strength of the war is gone; the cheek of youth is pale.
                                        Fragments of Ancient Poetry

LAUGHING GIFTBALL

Yule-wrapped in its resilient, mucusine box,
Laughing Giftball puts the bounce into Christmas.

Ergonomic Giftball comes guaranteed
For four hundred hours of muscle-toning playtime;

Should you wish to profit from Giftball for longer,
Send it for checking to our Isle of Lewis factory.

For safety, keep Giftball away
From liquid helium, elderly persons, or water.

In some countries Giftball's fluorescent coating
Triggers treatable allergies. If in doubt, phone our free Skinline.

Thrown incorrectly, Giftball can emit a tone
Occasioning nausea and infrequent anal bleeding;

However, when propelled at the correct velocity,
Giftball will not shatter into shrapnel-like, lancing shards.

If your Giftball comes with the Giftball Xmas Launcher,
This must never be pointed at people, brickwork, or animals.

Should the Giftball's cap become detached
Evacuate the area. Giftball's patent core

Constitutes a powerful, recognized defoliant
(World copyright protected). Laughing Giftball

May interfere with pacemakers, satellites, and rechargeable shavers,
Should not be ingested, inverted, or retrieved by dogs.

Avoid indoor use. For more guidance see our website
aa dot aa dot rgh

Thank you for choosing Laughing Giftball.
Keep these instructions with you at all times.

ZERO

Thank you for calling Heatheryhaugh Nuclear Arsenal.
If your main lust is for weapons of mass destruction
Please try our other number in Inverbervie.

On your touchtone phone jab one for details
Of bombs that kill crofters but leave brochs and megaliths standing;
Two for snug dumpsites; three for pre-owned

Atomic oddments with warranties for several years;
Four for rucksacks of fissile material;
Five will patch you through to Glencora Gillanders,

Anthrax buyer for the Loch Ness and Great Glen area;
Six for the Arsenal's renowned in-house distillery;
Seven affords highlights of our unusual safety record,

Reassuring callers we are sited in a remote location,
Though, should you wish to visit, pressing eight provides
Pibrochs from this area of comical natural beauty.

Nine connects you to our twelve-hour emergency helpline
(Not staffed on Sundays, Hogmanay, or New Year's Day).
If this extension is busy, please yell your number

So someone can ring back at a more convenient time.
Thanks again for calling H. N. A.
Slàinte! Do not press zero.

AMAZING GRACE

For having our bedroom door partially blocked
Through each recurrence of the outbreak
By the greyish screen concealing your improvised morgue;

For nightly, 2 a.m. fire alarms
Occasioning rainswept evacuation
Of toddlers to the Crag-Top Mustering-Point;

For replacement neck skin after application
Of locally-bottled midge repellents
Sold at your netted Reception;

For midges in the butterdish every morning,
Midges in the salad, and watching with the reading lamp
Swarms on your magnolia ceilings;

For endless conversations about septic tanks
Breakfast, lunch, and dinner, then that notice by the juice-tray:
OUR SEPTIC TANK IS NORMAL AGAIN;

For bringing stained blankets for the baby's cot
Three nights running, plus not pointing out
Yon electric trouser-press was live;

For disturbance caused by The Riggers' Ceilidh-bar
Below our room, and The Pibroch VIP
Helipad immediately above;

For these and other Highland hospitalities
We of the Lowland Ascetic Church
Are truly thankful. We have your names,

Your towels, your linen, your antique rugs,
Lead from your roof, your barman, your whiskies,
Your fuses. You'll be in our prayers.

I am an epileptic boy.
You must just call me John.
Papamamma are not allowed
To say I am their son.

Sometimes I heard my Mummy weep;
My Daddy stared at me.
I birled and fell and birled again.
I saw what he could see.

The Windsors hurt, but they are slaves,
Born into golden chains.
Their marriages are spied upon.
They got me for their pains.

I may not go. I cannot go.
I tear round this estate.
Dinging the wind and howling snow,
I prophesy, and wait.

I knight the bushes in the park,
I dream about the Tsar.
Will someone come and rescue me
Or will there be a war?

My head is full of guillotines,
Cannonballs and shot.
Lancers charge across my brain.
They're all the hope I've got.

So, dirty smug republicans,
Who think all royals do
Is eat quails' eggs and swallow port,
What do *I* say to you?

And you, the callous *status quo*
Of tub-fed monarchists,
Will you fall silent if you see
Red weals across my wrists?

I am the smashed winter elm,
The bomb, the Queen's depression;
I am the medicine cabinet
Forever locked in session.

I am the little prince who's lost,
The royal Peter Pan
Who sees what everyone denies
Simply because I can.

I am the knight behind the wall,
Felled in the noonday sun;
The day will come when my proud face
Is pecked by everyone.

I am Le Prince d'Aquitaine.
The gardeners call me John.
Great oaks will grow in Windsor Park
Long after kings are gone.

An angel swept with gelignite
Along the Royal Mile;
Each time she passed a boy in blue
She beamed her sweetest smile.

Her heels clicked on the cobblestanes
Sae regular, sae true
As if a wee toy soldier corps
Had held its ain Tattoo.

She full-beamed her hard, pinny eyes
Beneath her tartan snood,
And watchers at street corners rasped,
'Aye, there gangs Wendy Wood.'

Wendy chaps on a black door
Down a dank close late at night,
Chap! chap! chap! chap! Students inside
Start wide awake with fright.

'It's only me, lads, Wendy Wood.
I've brought a wee tan case.
Inside are all my private things.
Please keep it in this place.'

Before yon boys could answer back,
Sly Wendy slipped away.
The students laughed, went back to bed;
One a.m., Wednesday.

At two a.m. a lad jumped up,
His name Calum MacLean;
He peered once in Wee Wendy's case
And didnae look again.

Cool Calum caught the Irish boat,
Whistling a Gaelic song;
But down that Edinburgh close
Blue bobbies filed along.

They chapped upon the students' door,
'Good morning, folks, what's this?'
Yon Embro bobby gave that lad
A furious Glasgow kiss.

Two policemen snatched the wee tan case,
Held it against the light,
Slit it open with a knife
And out spilled gelignite.

'Yous lads are all under arrest,
Traitors against the crown.
Yous are bloody Scottish nationalists,
And you, son, are a clown.'

The lads were hauled down to the jyle.
One of them soon was deid.
Another whispered, 'Wendy Wood –
That bitch is aff her heid.'

Wild Wendy led a patriot group,
A tartan harpy pack,
Whose dragons' breath of rhetoric
Could torch a union jack.

They jobbied-up a pillar box.
They marched around the town,
Inciting, 'Who will volunteer
To burn Westminster down?'

Some hailed her as our Joan of Arc,
Some cried her Sleekit Hoor.
But one or twa whispered the words,
'*Agent provocateur.*'

One day she bayed for English blood,
The next she told a story,
All coy, top-drawer sweetness and light,
On TV's *Jackanory*.

What was the good of Wendy Wood?
Was the feather in her cap
Put there by MI6? and was
Her venom real, or crap?

The squaddie digging Wendy's grave,
Held no strong views on that.
The hole he dug was tight and snug.
For Scotland, that was that.

But some who visited her there
Maintain they heard a rap
On wabbit, rotting coffin wood,
Chap! chap! chap! chap! chap! chap!

IMPOSSIBILITY

IMPOSSIBILITY

Under the North Sea, a mile off Elie
Where once she was noticed in a mullioned window,
White lace cap rising, brooding over her table,
Margaret Oliphant Wilson Oliphant
Translates on to starfish and nacred shells
Montalembert's *Monks of the West*

Still weary, awash with hackwork to support
Dead Maggie, Marjorie, Tiddy, and Cecco,
Her water babies, breathing ectoplasm,
She watches aqualungs glow with shellac,
Mindful how she loves light's aftermath,
Protozoa's luminescent wash

On the Firth of Forth; she drifts
Eagerly shorewards, can almost touch
Piers at St Andrews, cybery, Chopinesque fingers
Of Tentsmuir Sands, Blackwood's Strathtyrum
Pressure-resistant, bathyscaphic den
Deeply upholstered with morocco books

Ich bin Margaret Oliphant
Je suis Margaret Oliphant
I am Margaret Oliphant
You are Margaret Oliphant
Vous êtes Margaret Oliphant
Sie sind Margaret Oliphant

I love my home, its *lares et penates*
Of broken shoe buckles, balls of green wool,
Needles, its improvisatory architecture
Feeding my work with interruptions, turns
Snatched, forty-winked; stashed seed pearls in a dish
Radiate homely, incarnational light

Sometimes the green walls glimmer, elverish,
Phosphorescent, spectrally alive,
Razorfish splay galvanized medium's fingers
Seeking burnished heads of polyps and carageen
Brocaded with plankton, nuzzled by antlered snails,
Vulval, brasslit, flecked and veined and washed

Dinner-suited Auchterlonian clubmen
Fill the fishtank windows of the R & A;
Subsea, in my dark, Victorian
Antimacassared, embroidered sewing room,
I'm inky, threaded with spectra, gynaecological
Eyeball thistle-tassels of the sea

Brown, blue-grey, single-cell-like
Pre-embryo materials in store
But never used, spermatozoic spirits
Haunt the sunned waters, seances of plankton lie
Paperweight-still, flower heads, floating marbles
Undulating in slow liquid glass

I am too antisyzygously Scottish,
Thirled to names like Eden, Wallyford,
Pittenweem; tidally to and fro
Mights and maybes captivate me, I waver
Between hot toddy and hard, cold-boiled chuckies
Smooth and rounded as a baby's skull

Oceans teem with informational currents;
Lord Kelvin's submarine telegraphy
Nets continents; minke whales, prawns,
Mackerel and reef-life hover, agog
Though bored by its contents: same old same old
Verisimilitudinous whine

When Alexander Diving Bell invented the xenophone
I heard his voice calling, 'The sea! The sea!'
Hollowly into a shell
As if he could contact Robert Louis Verne
Or all the impossible, massed, forlorn spirits
Edinburgh exiled, waving from twenty thousand leagues

Under force eights the Lusitania,
Hood, Tirpitz, Mary Rose lie barnacled,
Cell-like binnacles of another life
Lost to the world above but frozen here
Among squid, mantas, coral, nameless shoals
Writhing in a lurid, marine Somme

Is the sea Scottish? What are the oceans' flags?
Britannia is ash on the surface of the waves;
We commend   the deep
In   mem
Dot dot dot dash dash dash dot dot dot
          aere peren

Almost meaninglessly vulnerable
To men who hold them with incomprehension
Softened by love, small crania nestle in tweed
Until a woman comes, a maid, a nurse
With her efficient, separating smile
Allowing cigar smoke, whiskies, broadsheet papers

Breastfeeding women soldier
Lovingly, intimately, hurt
Night after night in private dawn campaigns,
Babies in regiments, the Royal Scots Greys,
The Fusiliers, the Guards, madonnas, children,
Waterloo, Sebastopol, Verdun

'Why me?' I cried when Cecco died, 'Why you?'
'Why you?' echoed St Andrews cliffs, 'Why me?'
Sounds of my voice and of my voice re-echoed
You-me, me-you sieved through the bells of flowers,
Merged with sea-urchins, stairwells, conches,
Telephoned through grasses, filtering inside

Hay stalks, through woods and coffee pots
Soundwaves of me and you acoustically
Married plunged beneath St Andrews Bay
Out among lobsters, creels, beneath the hulls
Of homing Fifies sailing by the stars,
Bonded, faithful, never-answered cries

Fed through bakelite receivers, new
Technologies of machines and genes, systems
Replicating, generating, creating
Heavens of sea-slugs, ganglion-by-ganglion maps
Linking you to me, me-you,
Cecco . . . I am dying to hear you

Caravans of beasts cross the sea floor
Battling; there should be more tomes like Forbes's
History of British Starfishes,
More unignorable music like my baby's
'Stennynennynennynennynenny'
Vibraphoned with the long pibrochs of whales

Next, we'll be remixed as a strange city
Where the dead one spring day are allowed
Visits to the living, but gilled under the waves
Where none can breathe, where riverine
Currents of cold meet a persistent Gulf
Stream, thawing a cryogenic, living flood

Sanctioning *in vitro* fertilization, I shoal
Cell by cell by cell by cell by cell
Teeming with breathless nanosecond fins
Deluged with algorithms, difference engines, mouths
Kneading me into new shapes – tendrils, snout-neb,
Gills – and, while this happens,

I write *Katie Stewart* and *The Quiet Heart*,
The Perpetual Curate, menstruate, conduct
Business by telegraph, crisscross Europe, trill
Coloratura Italian names for carp,
Starfish and flounders, chant to squid about
Cosi fan tutte, *Rigoletto*, Siena

Where my husband's buried and where I watched my baby
Die in my arms; I am pulverisingly
Penniless, fortunate, and very tired;
In the early hours, weathered by children's breathing,
Chapters drift up among sluggish cuttlefish,
I see the passing lights of hulls above

Dull skies hanging low, but to the East
Hints of clearness, the light on the Bell Rocks
And at Arbroath, I watched the water-snakes,
They moved in tracks of shining white,
And when they reared, their elfish light
Fell off in hoary flakes

I am my own autobiography
Drafted with children nibbling at the page,
Clamouring, immaturely loud, dividing
Concentration, some quick and some dead,
O Cecco, Tiddy, Maggie, Marjorie,
I extrude your names as wormcasts on Fife's shores

Writing underwater I can be
Protean with shimmer and cascade,
Waxy and oaten, tearful,
Ambered, leylined, Atlantean, coursing
Dolphin-nuzzled, keen and adjectival,
Never to be netted or ticked off

Sea-surges nurse and cradle with me, to-froing
Diaphragms of water laugh, lullabying caves
Gargle the ocean, articulating waves'
Propulsive jokiness coming and going in squirts,
Margaret Oliphant Wilson Oliphant,
I am, babies, I am

I am a pearl and Scotland is a pearl,
Chuckies on the beach, each one a pearl,
Mudie's Circulating Library's
Books turn to pearl, spill out across the floor,
Glasgow's dour drinkers' spit shines for an instant,
Skrechled, tubercular seed-pearl nebulae

Sea water is all starts, an embryonic
Florilegium of lucent drifts,
Pulling, insistent, ceramic-glazed but soft,
Filtering light in snaily, Pictish spirals,
Irises, fannings, anemones, blurred nodes
Unfurling in the tidal give and give

Ossianic, nacre-rich, transforming,
Oceanic, ram-stam, brooking no stop,
Nation-like, yelling and rallying,
Subsiding, calm and violent, perjink
Splashed across headlines, Scotland, Scotland, Scotland
Quartz-strewn, Laurasian, pre-continental

Soften and turn to me, and slowly flower,
Fresh irises, sea pinks, forget-me-nots;
I'll fade away, profound, forgotten, growing
Pearlier beneath the Arran sun
I'll rise to be my land's loveliest necklace
Of Margarets, scattered, spilling far wee stars

Dear Mr Blackwood, here is a short story
Dear Mr Blackwood, here is my *Kirsteen*
Dear Mr Blackwood, my review is finished
Dear Mr Blackwood, I enclose one lung
Dear Mr Blackwood, here is my baby's coffin
Dear Mr Blackwood, say that I am brave

Non-voices emerge from slush of tidal muds,
Pied and shaley, or from singing sands'
'   !'
Coming to me as a medium crying
Childishly, childlessly, for five lost children,
Sperm speckling agate, mealy discolourations,
Random, dark flecks held in tortoiseshell

C.V.: M. O. is born in Wallyford
Now her family moves to Liverpool
Now she suffers a broken engagement's silence
Now, twenty-one, she publishes a novel
Now she visits Edinburgh, woos Blackwood
Now she marries sad Frank who designs stained glass

Now she gives birth (a baby girl) in London,
Maggie, now a puir wee thing who dies,
Now a son dead after one long evening
Now another son, Etonian Tiddy,
Now a fifth child, Stephen (d., influenza)
Now Frank dies, now Cecco is born

Now Maggie dies, now Margaret drowns in novels,
Writing while her last surviving children
Play around her, or wave from a barouche's
Switzerland/Jerusalem/Eton/Balliol College;
Tiddy dies, then Cecco; she writes
'The Library Window', 'A Beleaguered City'

Where the dead brush lithely past the living,
Fussily depart, return, like trains
Depart, return, depart, 25 June
1897, Mrs Oliphant
Passes; I see her mobbed by lugworms,
Bass and elvers, 100% gleg

Dear Mr Murray,
                  Our language should be gendered,
Making the following proudly masculine:
Vending machines, trees, typewriter ribbons,
Cups, semolina, while we would still speak
Of ships as 'she', along with mathematics;
Some surprises too, as Italians say

Il soprano (masculine) or in France
Penis is fem.; then, my dear Mr Murray,
Talk would flow much more pleasurably through
Amniotic diction, a real heart-throb
Philology that swilled and swirled and sworled,
Aye your faithful savante,
                              Lover of Words

Since 'Margaret' = 'pearl', I love to dream
To Bizet's music of a great pearl fished
From Tay, or Spey, or tropical in flarelight
White with clams found by divers in the Gulf
Off Qatar deep in elephantine darkness
Surfacing with tiny globes of light

Some people hate my style's stop-start
North Sea sun-chill, a shoal veering away,
Sighted, lost, slyly looping back
In medias res; my life like yours is
Conch-shaped, a diagram of the human ear
Straining to catch my own repeated name

Sing me map references — long, measured numbers
Pinpointing sandbars on lined nautical charts
Telescopes and periscopes have checked;
Let me read materialist spirits,
The Theology of Oceanography,
Innumerable Worlds, The Birth of Life

Fallen in love with the capricious dirt
Of Scotland where a man's a man now I
Hymn angelfishes' aquadynamic hush,
Salmons' effort; my epithalamia slocken;
Sea erodes natural amphitheatres,
Sootily Glasgow slips beneath the waves

Trapped air bursts out of Sauchiehall Street rooms,
Bubbling wildly upwards, tenemental grime
Flakes off and masses on the inky surface;
All the streetlamps fizzle and go out
But on the seabed shops unlock their shutters,
Couples uncertainly begin to dance

Round the submarine telegraph; share prices,
Dates, loves, scientific formulae
Mingle and shine among briny, gum-eyed beasts;
Sea cucumbers, Reuters, brittle-stars,
Editions of my novels, comb-jelly, *The Times*
Recirculate through washed, clean, air-free rooms

Nothing is solid, schist, sandstone, and chert,
Ovoids of granite, rock anemones,
Light-beams' white spots on red serpentine –
All have been molten, flowed as softly
As the Kinness Burn, amber and carnelian,
Chalcedony, bud-petals of the earth

Open around me, a hard-won bouquet
Held in triumph in my own marquee
Ordered to celebrate full fifty years
Writing for *Blackwoods*; pert champagne corks pop
Slàinte! Cheers! Salut! MRS OLIPHANT REQUESTS
THE PLEASURE OF THE CREATURES OF THE SEA

Scotland has never seen democracy;
History: Red Comyn's wife's demeaning wail
Over her children, through rich, spirituous rain
Soaking a slaughter on imperial fields,
Pissed regiments; I want some dignity
For the unmaimed in a democratic land

Buy Mrs Oliphant's *The Chronicles of Carlingford*!
'An assured success' 'A work of great delight'
'Splendidly touching' 'A domestic jewel'
'Her translation of Montalembert will live forever'
Vellum 3 vols. Octavo First Edition
Come buy! Come buy! Come buy!

Father Almighty, I strive against thee;
I reproach thee; I do not submit;
Maggie, if you would but rap the table
Once, if I could but hear your quiver
In the medium's voice; routine starts up again;
Impossibly, Our Father, I endure

Pay me; I work; I will not be your necklace
Till you adorn me with creeled villages,
Arisaig, Morar, Crail, and Anstruther
Polished and strong, until I cast them off
One by one, slowly, in apocalypse,
Turning to wink then walk into the sea

Wee lovely, terrifying, imperious people,
Why did you die still in your knitted shawls,
Nursed, longed-for, fed? I'm crying
Over nothing, over an emptiness
Only I notice, my big, ridiculous name
Owling back to haunt your minute graves

I see a red-haired girl on the losing side
Always marching in a tartan toorie,
Skirt, strong shoes, down vennels of Scots towns,
Campaigning for democracy, my country
Right and wrong, she wears a cardboard breastplate
Proudly, with painted block caps, VOTES FOR WOMEN

Scotland, your Mary is a Margaret,
Shod in ultramarine, bangled with whelks;
Knox is my muse, his monstrous regimen
Landlubbed, declaiming on the Firth of Forth;
Non-swimmers' emblem, he wobbles, presbyterian,
Tiptoeing on chuckies; I pout him kisses of spume

Now the great winds shoreward blow,
Now the salt tides seaward flow;
Now the wild white horses play,
Champ and chafe and toss in the spray . . .
Children dear, was it yesterday
(Call yet once) that he went away?

Birth overbalances men, pitching them forward
A generation; balance-sheets slip from their hands
Pleasurably; a father birling round
Laughs to be ungainly, heavy-suited,
Dancing in the privacy of being with babies,
Emancipated, masculated, light

Roles for daddies: hedge-bearded, adamantine,
Fiercely crabbit, crouched behind their 'No!'
Or louche and yissless, slipping like a drink
Poured back down the bottle's green neck, spilt away,
Lost; I am a father and a mother
Underneath the waves of Pegwell Bay

Marriage: dappled light through red stained-glass
Gloving a limb, jewelling us, rich
Spectra coating and nacring everyday
Troubles: his tubercular, fathering voice,
'Now sleeps the crimson petal, now the white;
Nor waves the cypress in the palace walk;

Nor winks the gold fin in the porphyry font:
The fire-fly wakens: waken thou with me';
I woke in peeling, impasto Siena,
Frank gone; in hot, holy Jerusalem,
Frank gone; I am a single, married woman
Impatient with the surface of the earth

As the sea circles this planet's
Pictish spirals, Celtic solar discs,
World-snake popping its tail in its own mouth,
So I perfect my impossible, nuanced grit,
Nacring its pregnant shell, its given/giving
360°

SPIRIT MACHINES

in memory of my father,
Robert Alexander Nelson Crawford, 1914–1997

CD ROM

Play me a CD of roofless cols,
Towerblocks in a chutney-scented wind,

That gives up cuddies' stereophonic chewing,
Clydesdales nosebagged in cold hessian,

Noise of grapeshot entering a body,
Barley's will-o'-the-wisp kiss;

Compact Disc (Read-Only Memory)
Means I can never rearrange a sound,

Can't make the corncrake last a field longer
Or undo that gift of 'I do'.

Yon loved voice, faltering on the last high C,
Newborn, max-vol, needy yells

Still sound exactly as recorded,
Throwaway, absolute, unremixable,

Teasing the rapt ear forever.

TIME AND MOTION

You ticked a box for peeing on vitreous china,
Issuing a cheque, or ordering notes;
If your bus was late, a written explanation.
New regulations downsized conversation,
Making it tedious; forms asked each day
Please insert your personal number,
Then the survey moved on to another branch.

'Remind your staff that time is money' – moving
From hand to purse, from wallet to Geneva,
Auldhouse to Stirling, sterling-dollars, stocks
Traded for credit. Sharp, digital clocks
Beeped and shone, wee calculators flashing
Please insert your personal number.
Curved space was the milled edge of a half-crown,

But time birled slowly, an old spinning florin
Suddenly worthless, its long service
Abolished by the need to power ahead.
Clubby Edwardian offices were dead,
Crushed continental plates of Scots baronial.
Please insert your personal number
Between sheet steel and glass. The founder's statue

Darkened in a fibre-optic age
When money zoomed at light speed, or might idle
At phonecall-rate, then launch an e-mail panic.
Liquidity called up an oceanic
Tsunami of investment, cards demanding
Please insert your personal number
Through modems moving with no moving parts

24-hours. Lads axed the hardwood counters
Whose polished brass had ordered time to queue
Motionless, dark-suited and polite
With each day's takings to be banked that night.
Now nights and days were slurred by autotellers'
Please insert your personal number.
Girls in the toilets banked by mobile phone,

Each handset cloned from a *TV21*
I'd read in the corner waiting for my Dad
To stop for lunch, sweep up his hat, and take me
To the bank canteen whose Yorkshire pud would make me
Dream of *nouvelle cuisine.* Mouthing the words
Please insert your personal number,
I glared impatiently, zapped in from a future

Run by lean boys with VDUs, while Dad
Traitorously introduced me to his cronies
Whom my cool generation would replace
With cash machines. They vanished without trace
As we shook hands; soon they'd be reading
Please insert your personal number,
Abducted by aliens who all looked like me

And mumbled electronic dialect,
Gawping at prehistoric, stacked punched-cards,
And ran our lives through personal organizers,
Then met the old only to smirk like misers,
Sussing their personal pension plans, suggesting
Please insert your personal number,
And moved on fast because we hadn't time.

EXCHANGE

Promising always to pay the bearer, money aspires to the condition of purest spirit. Divesting itself of carnal assets, it sheds its own metal and metal-stripped-paper body. It passes like wild bees into the shadowy screen. In the silicate moonshine of e-mailed figures, money resurrects. The lilac bushes, the cypress alley, the wild brier: all are transactions, costed, sold on at a profit. Money takes the dim seas and genetic mapping, neural networks and rippling, running water; pours them through each other on the velvet shores of dusk. Money burns the body of everything, so it can become spirit, dreams and thoughts of money. Now shapeless itself, its body deferred forever, money promises all cybery shapes: an immortal form of star-eyed silence, a harsh white heron of exchange. In the Ossianic twilight woven with the shuttles of money screens of the world fade out and rekindle with light.

LIGLAG

It's sniauvin i the Howe o Alford;
Whaiskin liggars are wede awa.

A' wark's twa-handit-wark this season,
Screens daurk as a hoodie craw.

Torry-eaten databases
Yield scotch mist o an auld leid,

Bodwords, bodes, thin scraelike faces.
Peter an Major Cook are deid.

Nemms o places haud thir secrets,
Leochel–Cushnie, Lochnagar,

Luvely even untranslatit,
Cast-byes unnerneath the haar

Dreepin doon tae Inverbervie
When the haert's as grit's a peat.

Youtlin souns blaw frae the glebe.
Pour a dram an tak it neat,

Neat as Cattens, Tibberchindy,
Tomintoul or Aiberdeen,

Mapped an scanned, a karaoke
O gangrel souns I ken hae been

Mapread an spoken by my faither
I mony a cowpissed bield, a Bank

O Scotlan, or a Baltic dawn.
Skourdaboggie, auld an lank,

I key them intae this computer's
Empire by a taskit wa.

Peterculter, Maryculter.
Tine haert, tine a'. Tine haert, tine a'.

SENSATION OF ANOTHER LANGUAGE

It's snowing in the Howe of Alford; gasping violently for breath, salmon that have lain too long in the fresh water are weeded out. All work is second-rate work that needs redoing in this season, screens dark as a carrion crow. Databases that are like exhausted land give up the small but wetting rain of an old language, traditional sayings expressing the fate of a family, portents, thin faces like shrivelled shoes. Peter and Major Cook are dead. Names of places hold their secrets, Leochel-Cushnie, Lochnagar, lovely even untranslated, stuff thrown away as unserviceable underneath the sea-mist dripping down to Inverbervie when the heart is ready to burst with sorrow. Feeble sounds, like those of dying animals, come from the field by the manse. Pour a dram and take it neat, neat as Cattens, Tibberchindy, Tomintoul or Aberdeen, mapped and scanned, a karaoke of wandering sounds I know have been mapread and spoken by my father in many a shelter pissed on by cows, a Bank of Scotland, or a Baltic dawn. Like the last surviving member of a family, old and spare, I key them into this computer's empire beside a wall fatigued with hard work. Peterculter, Maryculter. If you let sorrow overcome you, you lose everything. If you let sorrow overcome you, you lose everything.

DEINCARNATION

Each daybreak laptops siphon off the glens,
Ada, Countess of Lovelace, Vannevar Bush,

Alan Turing spectral in Scourie,
Babbage downloading half of Sutherland

With factors and reels, inescapable
Whirring of difference engines.

Inverailort and Morar host
Shrewd pioneers of computing.

Digitized, blue, massive Roshven
Loses its substance, granite and grass

Deincarnated and weightless.
Shaking hands with absentees,

Beaters, gutters have their pockets emptied
Of any last objects, even a nanomachine,

A pebble, a lucky coin.
Skulking on Celtic Twilight shores,

Each loch beyond is cleared of itself,
Gaelic names, flora, rainfall

So close, the tangible spirited away,
Cybered in a world of light.

Blearily rummaging the internet,
Aged thirty eight, not knowing where I was,
I found a site designed as an old harled manse,

Sash windows opening on many Scotlands.
Through one surf broke on the West Sands, St Andrews,
And through another Glasgow mobbed George Square.

Templeton carpets fluttered up and clucked:
Crevecoeurs, La Fleches, azeels, minorcas,
Cochins, Langshans, Scots dumpies, Cornish game.

The hallstand's canny, digitized gamp
Pointed to fading pixels; when I touched them
I felt *The Poultry-Keeper's Vade-Mecum*,

Though in the next room, where a bren–gun spat,
Its title changed into *King's Regulations*;
Tanks manoeuvred round the hearth and range,

Smashing duck eggs, throwing up clouds of flour.
Fleeing the earth-floored kitchen, an ironing table
Hirpled like girderwork from bombed Cologne

Into the study where my Aunt Jean studied
How not to be a skivvy all her life,
While my dead uncle revved his BSA,

Wiping used, oily hands on Flanders lace.
Ministers primed themselves in Jesus's Greek.
Bankers shot pheasants. Girls sang. My father

Walked me through presses with a map of Paris,
Though all the names he used were Cattens, Leochil,
Tibberchindy, Alford, Don, Midmill.

I understood. 'Virtual reality?'
I asked him. In reply he looked so blank
His loved face was a fresh roll of papyrus

Waiting to be made a sacred text,
Hands empty as the screen where he projected
Slides of our holidays at Arisaig,

His body fresh cotton sheets in the best bedroom
Of his boyhood home before he was a boy.
Waiting here, he waits to meet my mother,

For a first date at St Martin in the Fields.
Here, his father, Robert, catches light
On his own deathbed, pipe and *Press and Journal*

Combusting in a way none can control.
Manse rooms huddle, fill with shetland ponies,
London tubes. There is no here. Here goes.

En te oikia tou Patros mou monai pollai eisin:
In my Father's house are many mansions:
If it were not so, I would have told you.